EAT LIKE A LOCAL- GERMANY

German Food Guide

Mikael Arcangeli

Cover designed by: Lisa Rusczyk Ed. D.
Image 1: Thorsten Hansen https://www.thorstenhansen.com/deutschland/

CZYK Publishing Since 2011.

Eat Like a Local

Lock Haven, PA
All rights reserved.
ISBN: 9798647094674

BOOK DESCRIPTION

Are you excited about planning your next trip? Do you want an edible experience? Would you like some culinary guidance from a local? If you answered yes to any of these questions, then this Eat Like a Local book is for you. Author Mikael Arcangeli offers the inside scoop on German cuisine. Culinary tourism is an important aspect of any travel experience. Food has the ability to tell you a story of a destination, its landscapes, and culture on a single plate. Most food guides tell you how to eat like a tourist. Although there is nothing wrong with that, as part of the Eat Like a Local series, this book will give you a food guide from someone who has lived at your next culinary destination.

In these pages, you will discover advice on having a unique edible experience. This book will not tell you exact addresses or hours but instead will give you excitement and knowledge of food and drinks from a local that you may not find in other travel food guides.

Eat like a local. Slow down, stay in one place, and get to know the food, people, and culture. By the time you finish this book, you will be eager and prepared to travel to your next culinary destination.

OUR STORY

Traveling has always been a passion of the creator of the Eat Like a Local book series. During Lisa's travels in Malta, instead of tasting what the city offered, she ate at a large fast-food chain. However, she realized that her traveling experience would have been more fulfilling if she had experienced the best of local cuisines. Most would agree that food is one of the most important aspects of a culture. Through her travels, Lisa learned how much locals had to share with tourists, especially about food. Lisa created the Eat Like a Local book series to help connect people with locals which she discovered is a topic that locals are very passionate about sharing. So please join me and: Eat, drink, and explore like a local.

TABLE OF CONTENTS

17. Reibekuchen
18. Falscher Hase (Fake Rabbit)
19. Apfelpfannkuchen (Apple pancakes)
20. Maultaschen (Dumplings)
21. Toast Hawaii
22. Sauerbraten
23. Asparagus with white sauce and ham
24. Kartoffelknödel (potato dumplings)
25. Senfeier (mustard eggs)
26. Sauerkraut
27. Zigeunerschnitzel aka (Politically incorrect) - "Gypsy schnitzel"
28. Eiersalat (egg salad)
29. Horse-meat Salami
30. Zwiebelkuchen (Onioncake)
31. Eisbein (Knuckle)
32. Bienenstich (Beesting)
33. Bienenstich (Beesting)
34. Heringssalat (Herring salad)
35. Jägerschnitzel (hunter's schnitzel)
36. Kartoffelsuppe (Potato soup)
37. Jagdwurst
38. Himmel und Erde (Heaven and Earth)
39. Kohlrabi
40. Rote Grütze (red fruit jelly)
41. Schupfnudeln (potato noodles)

READ OTHER BOOKS BY CZYK PUBLISHING

DEDICATION

This book is dedicated to my mother, and to my father. I simply would not have lived the incredible life that I have up to now if not for them...

ABOUT THE AUTHOR

Mikael Arcangeli (b. Michael Webb) is a professional artist, composer, writer, researcher, musical director, actor, concert pianist, producer, and food-lover who has entertained at least two former U.S. presidents, and once held the world record for the longest piano recital in history (32 hours). With 21 years of live worldwide performances and production experience to his credit, Mikael is a highly decorated and well sought-after entertainer. Mikael has a natural gift for setting the right vibes at a formal or informal event, gathering, or social scene as a proud "intro-extrovert". He currently resides in Hamburg, Germany with his wife, two adorable daughters, and two cats - Mika and Luka.

HOW TO USE THIS BOOK

The goal of this book is to help culinary travelers either dream or experience different edible experiences by providing opinions from a local. The author has made suggestions based on their own knowledge. Please do your own research before traveling to the area in case the suggested locations are unavailable.

Travel Advisories: As a first step in planning any trip abroad, check the Travel Advisories for your intended destination.
https://travel.state.gov/content/travel/en/traveladvisories/traveladvisories.html

FROM THE PUBLISHER

Traveling can be one of the most important parts of a person's life. The anticipation and memories that you have are some of the best. As a publisher of the *Eat Like a Local*, Greater Than a Tourist, as well as the popular *50 Things to Know* book series, we strive to help you learn about new places, spark your imagination, and inspire you. Wherever you are and whatever you do I wish you safe, fun, and inspiring travel.

Lisa Rusczyk Ed. D.
CZYK Publishing

Image 1: BAMBERG Germany - Thorsten Hansen.

*"I cook with wine. Sometimes I
even add it to the food."*

– W.C Fields

This book is written by me, yours truly -
Mikael Arcangeli. The main topics of
discussion in this writing are designed to help
you to eat like a German. I am an American. I am
not a naturalized German. I cannot consider myself
to be German in the literal sense. I do not look like a
typical German. I rarely even speak German. There.
I did it. I got it out of the way...Sheesh!

Now before you decide to chuck this seemingly
"sham" group of stories and recipes away in the
waste-basket and accuse the author of this book, me,
of being a fraud, I must tell you that I have lived and
worked in Germany, on the economy, for a pretty
long time up to this writing. My spouse of fourteen
years is German - East, Middle, and West. My
children both are born and raised in Germany and can
speak fluent German and American English since
they were born, or from early childhood. I was,
myself, raised in Germany from one to around six

years of age, as were my siblings, though I'm the youngest of the clan. The talk of German recipes, foods, and treats was a pretty standard topic in my household growing up, as were the culinary delicacies of many cultures and customs around the world. We were all proud U.S. Army brats. I've lived in Korea, visited Japan, Central Europe (there was no "East" Europe for me to legally visit as a youngster in my time, but I've been as far as Moscow as of this writing), and many other world nations by the time that I was already twelve years of age.

As a bonus, my stepfather was Dutch, my stepmother Korean, and lastly, I am a professional musician for over twenty-one years up to this writing. As a 'traveling man', I can assure you, the reader, that I may know a thing or two about the subject at hand – How To Eat Like A German - This is not as a result of having, "..been there, done that.", but rather that I have had a sincere interest in other cultures since as long as I can remember, and that the kindness and love of the German culture, in particular; it's people, it's music, it's art, it's sciences, it's ingenuities; I have a grand appreciation of Germany's true and proud #1 virtue: Love.

Furthermore, as an extra-added bonus, I also grew up for many years in the heartland of Pennsylvania - the most German, Dutch, Amish, Irish foods and delicacies in one state or city in the United States that I know of next to Wisconsin or San Francisco, the places where many Germans have also migrated to over the years. I tell you; it's shocking to see the same 'Nittany Lions' emblem logo crested across buildings in your little German town in the middle of nowhere, knowing that you used to see this same emblem plastered across labels, sports teams logos, clubs, and groups in your home town back in "good ol' PA".

Ironically, I'd say that the German and American taste-buds are strikingly similar given American history and it's overwhelming connections to Germany. Germany has had a historically massive influence on the United States since it's inception. Many connections between Germany and the U.S. exists other than the culinary arts throughout the history of these two proud nations, for example, notably "The Blue Book", written by Baron von Steuben, the man that helped organize and train the first rugged American troops of George Washington for battle through German and Hessian-warrior training methods and disciplines. I will not delve into a history lesson, because we all know that there are, literally, an endless amount of readily available resources that can far better attest to what I'm saying here about German and American relations. Speaking of, both my paternal and maternal grandfathers served distinguishably in WWII in the campaigns to liberate France and Germany from imperialism, and I'll never forget that, interestingly, both of my grandfathers had nothing negative to say, at least to me, about Germany, it's culture, or it's people. I only heard of positive, light, and charming details about the Germans from them, and I'm happy to keep my memory of them in this way.

German dishes are usually related to, among alternative things, deep-dish and hearty, meat-heavy dishes. This is often in part explained by the fact that Germany (Deutschland) is found comparatively far north and within the past, in laborious winter times, extreme care had to be taken to produce good food. There are, *"z. B."* (German abbreviation: "for ex."), many robust potato dishes. The pig is mostly considered a typically German provider of meats. However, this consideration will additionally apply to the kitchens of neighboring countries, like Danish,

Austrian, Polish, Czech, and Slovakian culinary arts. These criteria replicate a stereotype that may be applied to the larger cultural space of Central Europe. Comparatively, high-calorie desserts and tarts like the metropolis wreath and the timber cherry cake were long thought of to be typically German, as were candy and yuletide cookies, cakes, pepper haywire, stollen, and speculoos.

In the course of the economic process, immigration, and the stronger networking of Germany with others from every corner of the planet, the trends are more towards reduced meat consumption and connoisseur culinary art. There's the "rediscovery" of the lighter regional dishes that the earlier clichés concerning German culinary arts that are no longer applicable. Traditionally, the most highlighted meal of the day is lunch, anytime between noon and 3 p.m. The supper is sometimes a smaller meal, which frequently and solely consists of a couple of slices of good bread. In recent times, dynamical operating habits have led several Germans to eat their main meal in the evening.

The German breakfast consists chiefly of rolls, toast or bread with jam or honey, sausage or cheese.

Breakfast foods with milk, fruit, or any alternative farm-made merchandise is additionally standard, as is the hard or soft-boiled egg. Coffee, tea, juice, or cocoa with milk are at many times the best breakfast-drink of choice.

Beer is very standard, with all notable components, in most, if not all, European countries, particularly the Pils brand as a whole. Additionally, there are several famous regional beers, like Helles, Kölsch, Märzen, Altbier, Weißbier, or German Weisse. A nice and sparkling combination of brewage mixed with a fruit drink is termed "Radler" or "Spritzes" within the south of Germany, and "Alsterwasser" in the north.

Wine has become a glorious and worldwide tradition amongst many customs and cultures, though much of the 'wine' as we know it can trace its production roots and styles to... You guessed it - Central Europe! - with a history of sixteen famous wine-growing regions that are exceptional and distinguishable. This culture in Germany was started by the Romans around the 2nd century on the Moselle. The German wine comes chiefly from the areas on the Rhine, the Danube, the Main, the

Moselle, and the Neckar rivers. Riesling, Müller-
Thurgau (Rivaner), Silvaner, Spätburgunder, and
Dornfelder are the known German grape varieties.
The wine is additionally mixed with seltzer as a wine-
induced mixed drink.

Likewise, this style of drinkable wine (in the
southwest additionally known as 'Schörle') also serves
as an alternative fruit drink within the regions of
Rhineland-Palatinate, Saarland, and Baden-
Württemberg, which are associated with alternative
fruit growing areas and are once more in an upward
trend. This tradition, unbelievably, may be dialed
back as long as that of the wine itself. The
consumption of "strong drink" has declined within the
past decades; historically, liquor was consumed
primarily in northern European countries and later
within the working-class districts of the cities, with a
division being reached within the 19th century with
"potato strong drink" (cf. liquor plague). In
distinction, the consumption of mixed drinks like
alcopops and cocktails has been a bit exaggerated in
recent decades.

Coffee is additionally popular in Germany, not just
for breakfast, but also within the afternoon to go with

a stylish cake or pie. Tea is incredibly standard in the eastern geographic region of Germany. Another favorite - the effervescent (bubbly) drinking water mixed with fruit juices - the mixture of the 2, known as "spritzer", also with cola in combination with fruit drinks are very commonplace in Germany as non-alcoholic soft drinks. A combination of cola and orange fruit drink, or orange soda, is termed Spezi, and is a very popular one especially amongst the German youth and teens, for reasons that I cannot personally begin to comprehend! "To each, their own.", they say...

I cannot possibly emphasize in words to exactly how good German food actually is, and how tasty, warm, hearty, energizing, and savory it is to eat German food in Germany and abroad. German food has been with me for my whole life, as well as so many others, and I can assure you that when you read on into the pages of this book that you will start to get hungry. I think that I am starting to get hungry as I write this!

From here on in, let's just dive right in and have a look-read about this incomparable list of German delights that will have you, dear reader, eating like a German in no time flat. *"Es lebe Deutschland!"*

Germany

Berlin
Germany
Climate

	High	Low
January	37	29
February	40	29
March	48	34
April	57	40
May	67	49
June	72	54
July	76	58
August	75	58
September	67	51
October	57	44
November	46	37
December	39	31

GreaterThanaTourist.com

Temperatures are in Fahrenheit degrees.
Source: NOAA

1. RINDEROULADE (BEEF ROULADE)

For this customary meat dish, hamburger leg cuts are normally beaten with onions, bacon and cured cucumber and wrapped. Rouladen are typically presented with either potato dumplings or pureed potatoes and cured red cabbage. Simmered winter vegetables are another normal side dish. The sauce is a flat-out prerequisite to adjust the dish and is typically poured over the meat. Spätzle are a decent supplement to the dish since they absorb the sauce well. This dish was viewed as a dish for ordinary citizens. It is these days delighted in by numerous individuals as a happy dish. I have to agree with this estimation...it's quite good. You'll need:

The Roulade Meat

4–5 beef roulades

8-10 slices of bacon

2-3 onions

1–2 tbsp spicy mustard from Dijon

1 tbsp butter

2 tbsp clarified butter

freshly ground, white or black pepper

Sea salt or coarse salt from the mill

Sauce

2-3 onions

1/2 carrot

1/4 celeriac

1 clove of garlic

1 large tomato

1 tbsp tomato paste or a finished product from the trade

0.4 l beef broth, chicken broth, veal broth, vegetable broth, broth or cubed broth

1 sprig of thyme

1 bay leaf

freshly ground, white or black pepper

Sea salt or coarse salt from the mill

Preparation

Roulade

Strip the onions and cut them into rings with a slicer. Wash the roulades and pat dry with kitchen paper. Salt and pepper the roulades, brush with mustard and top with two cuts of bacon.

Spread the onions on top, crease the long sides a little over the filling, move them up and protect them with roulade needles or toothpicks. Or on the other hand, integrate it with kitchen string. Wrapping with blossom wire is simpler. (The wire must be exposed, not secured. Not appropriate for covered cookware.)

Wash the tomato under high temp water and quarter it. Clean, strip and de-bone the vegetables very finely. Let the fat become extremely hot, sauté the roulades overwhelmingly from all sides, salt, and pepper. Remove the roulades from the pan and pour off the vast majority of the fat.

Add the diced vegetables with the spread fry, the substance of the pot with tomato paste, tomatoes, and with the fluid deglaze. Use a wooden spoon to scratch the meal off the container base. Bring the sauce to the bubble and supplement the roulades. Add the hacked tomato. Let it move up once, and let it stew for around 1 hour and 50 minutes.

Season the sauce and season it as fundamental to your likings as possible.

2. BAUERNFRÜHSTÜCK (FARMERS BREAKFAST)

This hearty and healthy dish, which is regularly alluded to as "rancher's morning meal", was made as scraps dependent on singed potatoes and meat remains, which were blended and warmed in a skillet with everything else the fridge brought to the table. The dish may have become to some degree overlooked today, yet it is a prime technique for using every single imaginable remaining. It's bad to waste good food, so how about a nice stir-fry? For students with limited resources and limited amounts of cash, try and clear the fridge of everything that you thought you wouldn't like, put it all in the frying pan, and bear witness to German greatness, my friends... saving money with culinary efficiency.

3. KROKETTEN (CROQUETTES)

Everyone tends to love them and have forever favorited them, particularly mum´s home-baked potato croquettes!

It's truly not that troublesome:

1.5kg of potatoes, floury
3 eggs
four tablespoons of flour
1 tsp salt
one pinch of sugar
breadcrumbs

Cook the potatoes to mash them. Add the flour and eggs to the mashed potatoes, season with salt and sugar and blend everything well. Place the croquettes on a receptacle lined with baking paper. Bake at 200° C/392° F for about twenty minutes or until golden brown.

4. FRIKADELLEN (MEATBALLS)

Homemade meatballs might forever prompt the rest of the world of a childhood experienced in Germany, and therefore the inhibitions with that we tend to lordotic our hands into the chilled mass of meat for the primary time to form the meatballs. Frikadellen should not be confused at all with the Swedish meatball variation that has become popular for anyone outside of Europe that can make it to the long-awaited register of the IKEA, once they've fought through the long maze of kitchen appliances, make-believe entertainment systems, and baby beds.

For preparation, minced meat (usually mixed beef and pork) is mixed with egg and shredded and presumably, pre-steamed onions are added. Stale bread rolls or slices of toast are soaked in water, milk or cream so wonderfully ironed and kneaded into the meat mass. Breadcrumbs are typically used instead. Then, looking at the style, numerous spices like salt, pepper, parsley, marjoram and presumably nutmeg are mixed in. looking at the formula, garlic and mustard or caraway, as an example, also can be added. Then the mass is created into palm-sized flat bales that are cooked or cooked in hot fat. In Germany and Scandinavian nations especially, it's customary to show the bales in breadcrumbs before preparation.

Meatballs are served either as a plated dish with facet dishes or as a snack with mustard and rolls. With a changed formula, they found their means into the originally Yankee, currently international, aliment culture into what we all know and love as the hamburger. Remember what I said about the massive German influence in the USA since it's inception?

There are several names for part native and regional preparations like Frikadelle, Boulette, Bratklops, Fleischpflanzerl, Fleischlaberl, and Fleischküchle. The term Frikadelle has been employed in German since the tip of the 7th century.

5. KARTOFFELSALAT (POTATO SALAD)

I opt to keep one's hands off from the discussion of whether or not a truly delicious salad with vinegar-oil dressing or mayo should be served. As long as there are potatoes involved, for many Germans, then you know that everything is ok. The same could be said about sausages and bread.

In the northern components of Germany also as in Silesian and Bohemian culinary art, the salad is sometimes ready with a dressing containing mayonnaise. Pickled cucumbers or apples are usually added to the salad with mayonnaise within the Rhineland. Variants with apples and dishes dominate the north. In Germany, on the opposite hand, preserved cucumbers are combined with radishes or finely shredded onions. Roasted leftovers, 'matjes', sausage items and recent herbs also can be added to the dish as desired. Additionally, to mayo and mustard, boiled egg, preserved cucumbers, carrots, peas, and onions are some popular additions.

As an alternate to mayo, food preparation is additionally attainable, particularly in dietary culinary art. In Southern Germany and other European nations, the sliced potatoes are sometimes mixed with a broth made up of vinegar, oil, salt, pepper, and mustard. The dish also can contain shredded onions, cooked bacon cubes, garlic or cucumber slices. The marinade is commonly poured over the still-hot potatoes. The dish is then ready to serve and can be eaten hot ("warm potato salad") or cold.

Interestingly, in components of Styria and Burgenland, the salad is served with pumpkin seed oil. Chives are obligatory in Franconia.

6. SPÄTZLE

Spätzle never gets old! For many Americans, add melted cheddar cheese (many Europeans are not so privy to the "orange" cheese) and you will have the best alternative that one could imagine to good 'ol Mac 'n Cheese.

Spätzle and Knöpfle have a centuries-old tradition of production within the Swabian region of Germany and are of delicate importance for Swabian culinary artists. The Swabian literature is wealthy in poems associated with the "Leibgericht der Schwaben", as the literary work "Das Lob der Schwabenknöpfle" revealed within the timber courier in 1838, the literary work "Schwäbische Leibspeisa" or the

"Spätzles-Lied". This food is delicious enough to sing about!

The tradition of creating spätzle in Swabia may be traced back to the 18th century. In 1725, the Württemberg counselor and private medico Rosinus Lentilius combined "Knöpflein" and "Spazen" as, "...everything that's made up of flour." At that time, spätzle was widespread within the Swabian-Alemannic area; it's an associate and easy grain that thrives on poor soils. Spätzle flour contains heaps of glue; the dough works well while not with the addition of eggs.

Spätzle are historically scraped by hand, and hand-scraped spätzle from the board - additionally called 'board spätzle' - are still thought of as a special seal of quality to the present day. The native author Sebastian Blau (pseudonym of Josef Eberle) raised spätzle as a logo of the regional identity of the Swabians: "... the spätzle are the inspiration of our culinary art, the celebrity of our country, ... the be-all and goal of the Swabian menu ...".

Several exhibitions document the normal information in regard to producing within the Swabia region from its beginnings to the current time. The importance of spätzle for Swabian culinary art is incontestable by the novel "The Story of the Seven Swabians", that was first revealed in 1827, in step with that there's a habit in Swabia that you, "...eat 5 times each day, 5 times soup, and doubly knöpfle or spätzle". The earliest recipes for spaetzle are found within the Göppingen cookbook (see in literature) since 1783, which was written by Rosina Dorothea Knör, unmarried Schmidlin, née. Dertinger (1733-1809).

7. LEBERKÄS` (MEATLOAF)

"Leberkäse im Brötchen": a specialty that reminds the people of the USA of German Christmas markets especially, though additionally often found in an area rich with native German folks. Leberkäs` has been created in the Bavarian province for over two hundred years and has long been thought of as a classic in Bavarian culinary art.

Leberkäse means that "leftovers are within the box", that capably describes the assembly of the usual merchandise. The name Leberkäse (liver cheese) is usually deceptive as a result that liver cheese originally had no relevance to the liver organ. Leber is originally derived from recent German-language laiba, which implies and rests also as an immediate derivation of "laif" for a loaf, which comes from a similar word context. The suffix 'käse' may be an idiom variant for crates (see additionally: Engl. - "case").

8. GRÜNKOHL KASSLER UND KOHLWURST (KALE WITH SMOKE-CURED PORK AND CABBAGE SAUSAGE)

A tasty and hearty winter dish like mother used to make is kale. Many of you reading this might know these as 'collards', or ironically pronounced as "kah-la greens" to many from the south to the mid-southeastern United States. I still pronounce it this way to this day. To style with smoke-cured pork, cabbage sausage or each. Ale consumption may be a custom in large components of northern Germany and, therefore, Germany also has added in components of Scandinavia. Kale (locally known as brown cabbage) was harvested earlier than when the primary time of year is cold enough to produce frost, the bitter substances contained in it are then neutralized. Historically, Christian holy days before Easter was the tip of the kale season. Today, newer breeds are used, which may be harvested from September when there's milder weather with no frost.

Traditionally, a winter cabbage dinner in the company is preceded by a "cabbage tour" (cabbage tour or kale hike). This is often sometimes associated with any excursion through nature to the destination of the hotel wherever the food is served. My father used to quip to me and to the many Germans and locals that came through our household to eat or have a good drink that the actual purpose of the long strolls alone through the woods after an evening of eating cabbage was for a more obvious and "natured" reason that I will omit from this writing, and I will leave it up to your illustrious imagination. When nature calls...

Throughout the hike, the participants make merriment with local games like Boßeln or Klootschießen. Adequate alcoholic beverages are carried in an exceeding go-cart to strengthen and to guard one's self against the customarily frigid temperatures.

In the hotel or inn, the group serves medium kale, either thickened with buckwheat groats, oat groats or oat flakes or not, depending on the region, with (slightly caramelized) cooked potatoes or poached potatoes. 'Pinkel' is the characteristic insert within the area around Bremen and within the Oldenburger Land, whereas 'Bregenwurst' is within the region around Hanover, Hildesheim, and Magdeburg. These sausage specialties are typically and solely created in winter and for the preparation in kale and are rather uncommon in alternative regions. Additionally, standard as ingredients are smoke-cured sausage, cabbage sausage, (fresh) sausage, smoke-cured meat ends, bacon, or pork cheek.

The inexperienced cabbage meal culminates within the proclamation of the 'cabbage king' or the 'cabbage king couple'. Numerous strategies are used for the award of royal dignity. Either the amount of parts of every participant is evaluated, the load of the participants before and when the meal is decided, or the results of the games on the move are evaluated in step with secret and relaxed criteria. The cabbage king is the one who leaves the table last. It's up to the king or royal couple to prepare the kale meal of the subsequent year. Famous inexperienced cabbage meals manifest themselves, as an example, with the "Green Cabbage Connoisseur Festival" within the Hamburg Fish Auction Hall and with the "Defftig Ollnborg Gröönkohl-Äten" near Berlin.

9. LINSENSUPPE (LENTIL SOUP)

Especially in winter, this is a hearty and extremely delicious soup. It is 'de facto' good! Lentils are one in all the primary cultivated vegetables and stews with this legume are from the Babylonian culinary arts from around 1700 BC. Early change of state recipes for lentil stews may be found around 200 A.D. within the outgoing ancient Ellas at Euthymus and within the first century AD at the Roman connoisseur Apicius. Compared to alternative foods, lentils were comparatively cheap in the least times and, consequently, lentil dishes were still thought of as "poor food" back in the Middle Ages.

In some modern German regions, lentils are served with sliced blood pudding, extra vinegar, and sugar for seasoning in step with personal style. Alternative common facet dishes are smoke-cured meat, cracked sausage, bockwurst, Bregenwurst or Wiener sausages, and, additionally, Frankfurters. With the Swabian lentils with spätzle, the lentils are made ready with a bit of liquid as a vegetable addition.

10. SCHWARZWÄLDER KIRSCHTORTE (BLACK FOREST CAKE)

Interestingly to me, the American variant of this superior treat was always uppermost in my mind concerning the 'German chocolate cake" that I'd become accustomed to. I'm speaking of the one with coconuts and brown sugar with caramel added. I discovered as an adult that the true and authentic German chocolate cake par excellence is the "timber cherry cake", otherwise known as the German "Black Forest" cake.

A timber cake might be a cream cake that has to lay claim to its origins chiefly being in Germany since the 1930s and has become the foremost standard German cake over time. Nowadays it's thought of as the classic German cake and is regarded everywhere on the planet. The essential elements are chocolate biscuits lightly soaked with flavored cherry water, a flavored cherry filling, cream, cherries, and chocolate grated decorations. the precise origins of this are unclear, and they're not essential to be found within the timber.

Since 2006, the "Schwarzwälder Kirschtortenfestival" has been happening in Todtnauberg, a locality of Todtnau within the timber, wherever amateurs and professionals contend against one another with their home-baked timber cake in two competitive categories.

11. KOHLROULADEN (CABBAGE ROLLS)

Looking to do wonders to your immune system? These hearty cabbage rolls are significantly standard within a certain time of year (yes, that time of year that includes the sniffles), once the cabbage is seasonal and might be bought recently. The essential preparation for vegetable leaves stuffed goes back to the culinary arts within the geographic area.

Cabbage rolls, cabbage sausage or cabbage wrap are a dish that's significantly common in Europe and West Asia, consisting of cabbage leaves stuffed in several variations, that are medium, steamed or cooked.

In the variants common in Germany, head cabbage, white cabbage and, additionally seldom, red cabbage leaves are blanched so many leaves are placed on high of every alternative. These are wrapped around a powerfully seasoned meat mass made up of minced meat, bacon, onions, salt, pepper and, depending on your style, some marjoram and tied with a room thread or placed alongside roulade needles or picket skewers (including toothpicks). They are cooked in an exceedingly light meat broth at medium temperature till the sauce is creamy and aromatic. in step with some recipes, the filling will still contain rice or the sauce fixings and bacon. The same old dish is poached potatoes or mashed potatoes.

12. KÖNIGSBERGER KLOPSE

When I was a child, my siblings and I could not get enough of this originally East Prussian specialty. If you would like to let your meatballs contend with Grandma's, then take a glance at this formula and create these delightful meatballs at home. If you have children, they will thank you...trust me. I find myself at times still clamoring up to my significant other like a little whiney boy that's asking his mother what's for supper.

Königsberger Klopse meatballs, additionally bitter meatballs, caper meatballs or sauce meatballs are associated with East Prussian specialties made up of medium meatballs in bechamel with capers. they're named when the previous capital and royal town of Königsberg and therefore the East Prussian word for "small dumpling".

They are ready from minced meat or beef and pork with shredded anchovies (if salt herring is employed, the term herring pork was accustomed), onions, egg, and spices. The mass shaped into balls is medium in salt-cured water (possibly with vinegar or white wine) with onions, peppercorns, allspice and laurel, the sifted change of state broth is then certain with a bit lightweight mixture, cream, and ingredient and supplemented with juice and capers. Boiled potatoes or mashed potatoes are served as an accompaniment; in some areas, preserved beetroot is additionally common. Rice is additionally and widely used as a dish.

In 1845 Königsberger Klopse were delineated as follows:

"½ weight unit of weighed beef and 125 g of weighed pork are mixed well with a pair of eggs, 1 soaked, well-expressed milk bread, a couple of weighed anchovies and a bit crushed pepper. Finally, combine in grated bread rolls and spherical dumplings. Then prepare light flour from a pair of spoons of butter and flour, add a cup of boiling water and let a creamy sauce boil. Add a pair of tablespoons of finely weighed anchovies or a well-watered, finely weighed herring to the sauce, also as a couple of slices of lemon and a pair of tablespoons of capers; once everything is boiling, you'll be able to style the sauce with pepper, sugar, and acetum. ... "

In 1930, beef and pork, medium-cooked in salt and vinegar water, was the essential formula. The sauce was then mixed with flour and soured cream and alloyed with eggs and butter. According to a survey by the Forsa Institute in Germany, Königsberger Klopse have the best recognition among regional courts with 93%.

13. STRAMMER MAX

A simple dish that's created quickly, even when the time is brief. And, boy, if there were ever a dish that had extra meaning to its name, then read on with caution! We are all adults...hopefully. Simply unfold slices of bread, add butter, add a slice of ham and, at last with cooked eggs. At my home recently, slices of tomato and a small indefinite amount of mayo were placed underneath the egg... Delicious!

In a variation, some with completely different names like Strammer Moritz, Strammer angler fish,

Stramme Luise or Strammer Otto, the raw ham is replaced by liver cheese, sausage, or a variety. The expression "Strammer Max" was created around 1920 in Saxon that, quite literally, translates to a male human body part; the knowledge that might bring forth a childish little chuckle within us all - "Strammer Max" literally translates to "erect penis" - so transferred to the court. "The more you know...", they say?

14. HÜHNERFRIKASSEE

Hühnerfrikassee (Chicken Fricassee or french Fricassée American-style poulet) may be an extremely popular dish particularly for youngsters, however, it's additionally enticing for adults. I would argue against age discrimination when it comes to this dish or any similarly delicious delight. There are innumerable variants with vegetables like asparagus and peas.

In the past, dark ragouts with poultry, meat, fish or vegetables were additionally remarked as fricassee; for the 7th century, ingredients like liver, calf's feet, chickens, pigeons, apples and asparagus were documented. Likewise, one uses the name for similar dishes made up of steam, not seared, white or pork, edible fish or vegetables in an exceeding sauce certain with the ingredient. The dish may be copied underneath this name in German and French writings until the 18th century.

For the preparation of a classic fricassee, the meat or poultry is cut or divided into bite-sized items, gently laced in butter, dusted with flour and steamed in meat or chicken stock. The ensuing fund is alloyed with cream and ingredients and seasoned with white pepper, mace, and juice. Alternative ingredients may be sweetbreads, mushrooms, young peas, asparagus, morels, tiny onions, cauliflower, pistachios or capers. The sauce also can be added with cold butter. Rice is sometimes served as a side dish. Nothing can beat chicken and rice, one of the best combinations of foods known to man and woman.

15. GRAUPENSUPPE (BARLEY SOUP)

This is a German soup classic that may be enriched with all types of vegetables and warms up any occasion extremely well once it storms and rains outside. I live very close to Hamburg, and it is very seasonally rainy in a similar vein to Boston or any highly cultured port-city. This dish is a welcome addition to this aforementioned situation. 'Blauer Heinrich' (blue Henry) is a popular name for a barley soup. An explanation of this will be found within the wordbook of German conversationalists. After that, the term 'Blauer Heinrich' comes from the time of King Friedrich Wilhelm I of Prussia. The poor director appointed by the king was purportedly known as Heinrich. Throughout his time, awful skinny soups were distributed to the poor in metal bowls.

The term 'Blauer Heinrich' was additionally used for groats soup ready with skim milk. With this background, the employment of terms in photos and texts by Heinrich Zille is to be understood as once feeding the poor.

16. GRAUPENSUPPE (BARLEY SOUP)

This is a German soup classic that may be enriched with all types of vegetables and warms up any occasion extremely well once it storms and rains outside. I live very close to Hamburg, and it is very seasonally rainy in a similar vein to Boston or any highly cultured port-city. This dish is a welcome addition to this aforementioned situation. 'Blauer Heinrich' (blue Henry) is a popular name for a barley soup. An explanation of this will be found within the wordbook of German conversationalists. After that, the term 'Blauer Heinrich' comes from the time of King Friedrich Wilhelm I of Prussia. The poor director appointed by the king was purportedly known as Heinrich. Throughout his time, awful skinny soups were distributed to the poor in metal bowls.

The term 'Blauer Heinrich' was additionally used for groats soup ready with skim milk. With this background, the employment of terms in photos and texts by Heinrich Zille is to be understood as once feeding the poor.

17. REIBEKUCHEN

Do you feel guilty for not going to the gym for weeks or months? Years? No setbacks allowed, so simply bulk up for it by deciding to prepare potato pies for the whole family. In the first ten minutes of preparation, when the beginning of the rubbing starts, you just might see what I mean…

The main ingredient is in the raw and grated potatoes. Then the mass is gently squeezed out and mixed with chicken egg and flour to create a skinny dough. The batter, seasoned with salt and nutmeg, is then baked into bread in hot fat. Recipe variations include the addition of oatmeal, onions, bacon cubes, low-fat curd cheese, buttermilk, garlic, marjoram, parsley, salmon or other alternatives. They are just glorious.

Depending on the region, potato pancakes are eaten with some side dish that is alternatively sweet or made with salty ingredients. It's common to eat them with apple sauce or sugar. In the Bergisches Land, within the Münsterland, and in the Rhineland, they're additionally placed on buttered pumpernickel or eaten with beets, apple cabbage or jams. In Bavaria, this is additionally used as a dish, in components of the Saarland, in northern Rhineland-Palatinate, and for the winter, a bowl of soup is made up of the inexperienced beans. In the south of Germany, you'll be able to additionally eat leek vegetables with items of smoke-cured meat.

18. FALSCHER HASE (FAKE RABBIT)

For a delicious meatloaf or faux rabbit, minced meat is first mixed with soaked bread or breadcrumbs, also as egg, onions, salt, and pepper. several ancient recipes additionally contain hard-boiled and whole eggs as a filling. The mass is then formed into a loaf and first cooked, and at last medium-cooked to the tip in the oven or on the stovetop.

The names 'Falscher Hase' (false rabbit) or 'pretender' (hypocritically pretend) come from a while back from the copper or stuffed rabbit pans and roasters during which meatloaf has been baked in the past centuries. However, it was additionally common to "shape" a hare by hand or to grant the meatloaf known as "false hare" in the form of a hare's back. Most copper rabbit shapes and rabbit cooking pans are believed to have fallen victim to the war metal collections throughout WWI.

The term "Falscher Hase" (also "Polish Hare") was documented in cookbooks from the middle to the last half of the 19th century.

Falscher Hase is served in slices with the sauce and poached potatoes, and Switzerland nearly always with mashed potatoes or Hörnli (a pasta kind consisting of tiny, snaky tubes). Served cold it may be used as a chilly cut.

19. APFELPFANNKUCHEN (APPLE PANCAKES)

Apple pancakes are a preferred dish among youngsters in Germany. As an adult, I sometimes like to imagine apple pancakes as a cold snack to pack and eat like an in-between to supper, or a nice late-night leftover to help me while I binge on Netflix without a hunger hangover.

Whether for Sunday breakfast or as a daily snack, apple pancakes ought to land on international plates much more than they do up to now. You will need:

2 eggs, separated
one pinch of salt
one pinch of sugar
125 g of flour
½ tsp leaven
125 mil milk
125 mil drinking water
1 apple
oil

Peel and core the apple and take tiny items or skinny slices. Mix the egg yolks with salt, sugar, flour, leaven, milk and drinking water with the hand liquidizer, beat the egg whites until stiff and fold in. Finally, fold within the apple items fastidiously.

Heat the oil in an exceedingly warm pan and bake the pancakes till they're nicely brunette on each side. If you wish, you'll be able to sprinkle the pancakes with cinnamon and sugar. This is one of my personal favorites.

In distinction to the typically French 'crepes', pancakes sometimes have a lower amount of liquid and an even better egg or flour content, which makes the dough considerably thicker. They are additionally baked darker (with the assistance of sugar within the dough).

20. MAULTASCHEN (DUMPLINGS)

These are very good, and most importantly, very filling! You do not need much of this dish to satisfy a 'Hungry Jack' in the kitchen or dining room. Dumplings come back from the Swabian culture and include dough with a basic filling of meat, onions and soaked bread rolls or additional eater fillings, which permit you to use vegetable leftovers from the refrigerator before they deteriorate.

Depending on your preference, Maultaschen may be collapsable or rolled. a bit of water or macromolecule binds the food dough higher along and prevents the dumplings from exploding open. With a picket spoon handle, individual dumplings are divided to bring to an end.

The dumplings are cooked in boiling salt-cured water or broth. From there they're ready and added to what will soon become an empty dish.

Maultaschen are sometimes served in one in all the subsequent ways:

- In a broth as a soup inlay.
- "Malted", i.e. doused with onions cooked in brunette butter, and there's usually a salad.
- "Roasted", here the dumplings are made into strips so cooked within the pan (also with onions and/or egg).

The origin of the word "Maultasche" goes back to the 16th century and is first authenticated within that means as "Ohrfeige" ("slap in the face"), most likely because of the swollen form, like a nobleman's face may have appeared after having been challenged to a duel in the old 'gentlemanly' ways of old Europe. Another attainable rationalization is that it resulted from the recent long "a" from the word "mahlen" (to grind) as a Swabian idiom peculiarity, prepared in a bag with ground contents. Another rationalization within the vernacular refers to the place of origin within the Maulbronn religious residence. A Maultasche is so merely a shortened name for a Maulbronn-Tasche.

Maultaschen, or dumplings, are currently called a specialty as far as the farthest side of the Swabian borders.

21. TOAST HAWAII

This is a super straightforward student meal that has sugared many a collegiate evening. Toast a slice of bread, lace with ham and a slice of pineapple, bake in the oven with cheese and the magic is completed.

The invention of Toast Hawaii is mostly attributed to the old television cook Clemens Wilmenrod, who first introduced it in Germany in 1955.

On the show, Wilmenrod turned to the camera with a knife and aforementioned that he was the creator and may ne'er unfold the rest, otherwise, he would come by in person. However, Wilmenrod presumptively adopted the formula from his contender and teacher Hans Karl Adam. Cooks are like composers, who are like young mother lions - "Something happens to my creation, then something happens to you!"

Please put the knife down and step away slowly, Mr. Wilmenrod...

According to scholar Petra Foede, it should be a variant of the grilled "spam-wich" that's very widespread in the United States and has been slightly custom-made to German conditions and preferences. Foede's formula uses spam (breakfast meat) rather than medium-cooked ham and cubed cheese rather than a slice of cheese, however, it doesn't dissent otherwise. The formula was first revealed in 1939 within the formula folder.

22. SAUERBRATEN

This delightful and traditional dish gets its distinctive style and tenderness by marinating for many days in an exceedingly tempered vinegar-containing marinade. Be careful...this may be the most comprehensive and scientifically prepared dish of this book.

The meat is first placed in a marinade of vinegar, water or wine, onions, carrots and spices like laurel, clove, peppercorns in cool conditions for many days. Historically, the roast to be marinated was kept within the cellar at most 12° to 14° C/ 53.6° to 57.2° F. New and trendy hygiene laws solely enable storage temperatures within the lower single-digit home in the line trade. Science, remember? The meat should be dried fastidiously before preparation, otherwise, it can't be cooked well. When searing, the meat is quenched with the marinade and full of stock or water to cook. The sauce is flavored with a sweetener. Dumplings, food, and the dish as an example are counseled as facet dishes.

A selection of well-known variants is Rhenish, Baden, Swabian, Franconian, Saxon, Dresden, Westphalian and Thurgau dish. The dish Emmentaler Art is termed 'Suure Mocke' in Berndeutschen. This is applied additionally to beef and horse meat, pork, rabbit or other gamey meats that are seldom served as a dish.

23. ASPARAGUS WITH WHITE SAUCE AND HAM

Asparagus season is well known extensively in Germany, especially in the southwest region in my old town of residence - Schwetzingen. It was a true thrill and an even greater opportunity for me to play piano concerti of great composers like Ludwig van Beethoven and George Gershwin in Schwetzingen's immortally famous "Schwetzingen Schloß" (Schwetzingen Castle). What makes these memories the most remarkable to me is that I never could have ever imagined that I would play at the same castle that the incomparable "wunderkind" Wolfgang Amadeus Mozart did long ago where he once performed and entertained the aristocracies at the tender age of seven. When I think about this dish, the Schwetzingen Schloß easily comes to my mind since this dish is served there seasonally, including a yearly festival in the town of Schwetzingen that is crazy about the many varieties of asparagus dishes that are common there.

There are several artistic recipes with white and inexperienced asparagus, however, the classic is with poached potatoes, ham and home-baked sauce. In the region around the Lower Rhine, asparagus is additionally eaten with liquified butter and disorganized eggs, within the same geographic area with breadcrumbs cooked in butter. As a variant, a cooked meat Wiener schnitzel is additionally served with the asparagus; the mix of asparagus with cooked or steamed fish has been gaining in popularity for around the last twenty years. In Baden, asparagus is served with patties or scratches (Schmarrn) and medium ham. All around the urban centers, asparagus is sometimes served within the style of an asparagus dish made up of whole, medium sticks with coarse, Franconian sausages or tiny local sausages. In South Tyrol, Bolzano sauce is common, a sort of mayonnaise made up of poached eggs. In some regions of Schleswig-Holstein, asparagus is additionally eaten with "sweet" (over-polished) jacket potatoes. These jacket potatoes are medium-cooked and in the raw peeling once more in a frying pan with butter and sugar, served with diced ham and white sauce.

24. KARTOFFELKNÖDEL (POTATO DUMPLINGS)

As the name suggests, potato dumplings, or simply just dumplings, include a mass of potatoes that are formed into balls, boiled or steamed in saltwater. Kartoffelknödel or Kartoffelkloesse, in the province of Reibeknödel, in Schwaben Gleess and Gneedl, in Franconia Gniedla or Klüess and Germany, Erdapfelknödel are dumplings made up of poached potatoes or a combination of raw and poached potatoes (Thuringian dumplings) or a combination of raw potatoes and a floured dish (so-called Vogtland dumplings) are delightful.

In some recipes, dumplings made up of raw and medium potatoes, as an example, are known as semi-silk dumplings. There are many various recipes. Within the case of a recipe, the potatoes are cooked the day before and ironed through a potato press or a rough sieve or the raw ones are grated, mixed with a bit flour and salt, egg, to a firm dough and cooked in hot saltwater until they rise to the surface. The dumplings may be full of 'staff of life' cubes cooked in butter before a change of state.

25. SENFEIER (MUSTARD EGGS)

Senfeier or eggs in mustard sauce most likely come from northern Germany, from wherever they need to cover giant components of Germany as cheap dishes. We tend to not care however these mustard celebrations have landed on our plates as long as it is time for their comeback here, there, and everywhere. They are THAT good.

Senfeier, or 'mustard eggs', are a dish that has been passed down at a minimum of since the first 19th century. Henriette Davidis noted it in her sensible cookbook from 1845 in two forms: First, eggs with sauce, during which case the sauce was poured over the soft-boiled associated cut eggs and eaten as a snack or as an accompaniment to meat or bread. In distinction, she delineates it in an exceedingly completely different means for the daily table with sauce and potatoes and pickles. Betty Gleim additionally came with the concept of Senfeier in her Bremen cookery book. Additionally, to the historical recipes, eggs in sauce or with sauce are often found in trendy cookbooks of classic and culinary art.

26. SAUERKRAUT

To quote the film Spiderman 3; Harry Osborn - "You knew this was comin', Pete!"... Now we all knew that this food would make it to the list. England - Fish 'n Chips. Italy - Spaghetti. Germany - Sauerkraut. Have you ever actually soured a dish yourself? The advantage is clearly that you simply will add your favorite spices by the can and exponential fewer vitamins are lost. it's truly quite straightforward, though you only would like a bit patience...

Sauerkraut was one in all the most ingredients processed in the winter in Germany, The Netherlands and Poland up to the institution of newer conservation strategies. It additionally found its means into 'soul' culinary art. Heaps of this dish are eaten, around the world. Because of its high vitamin content (especially vitamin C), it prevents immune deficiency symptoms in winter. That's why it was used all year round as a provision in seafaring when it was discovered within the 18th century that the consumption of this dish prevented scurvy.

During WWI, this dish was renamed 'liberty cabbage' within the U.S., particularly throughout the Second World War, the stereotyped term 'Krauts' for Germans was usually employed in the English-speaking world, that is perhaps because of the historically high consumption of the dish throughout the winter months in Central Europe, particularly in Germany.

Sauerkraut is steamed with a bit of water or broth and associated fat for about a quarter of an hour. Common spices are - besides salt and pepper - laurel, juniper, caraway, cloves, marjoram, additionally tarragon, fennel seeds, savory or sugar. Looking at the region, ingredients like onions, apples or grapes are also additional. In Hesse, as an example, it's fruit juice, and in other geographical areas of Germany, it's beer. In some regional kitchens, a small bond is formed in Silesian culinary art by a couple of poached potatoes; tiny amounts of grated potatoes are also added to the herb in southern provinces. Sauerkraut dishes have an overwhelming regional diversity. The subsequent examples are employed well in communicative countries. For the 'Wellington boot ribs' with cabbage, the preserved pork chop is medium in the dish.

Sauerkraut is a very important part of Bavarian culinary art, principally seasoned with caraway seeds. Sauerkraut is additionally a part of the Swabian culinary art. The Filder areas south of the urban center are one in all the known areas for growing pointed cabbage (Filderkraut). The Filderkrautfest is well known each year in Leinfelden-Echterdingen. Bacon with the dish and Schupf noodles is additionally typical of Swabian culinary art. Sauerkraut is also commonly served as a dish in Berlin and geographic to the area as significant culinary art. In Franconia, the dish is medium-cooked many times. These provide a very robust style.

Sauerkraut in Germany is analogous to Franconian, however, it is commonly seasoned with additional caraway seeds. Throughout the southern communicative space, it's served as a slaughter plate with kettle meat and poached blood and liver sausages. In Germany, it's a part of the farmer's feast with cooked and salt-cured meat (or pork roast and smoke-cured meat), frankfurters and dumplings.

In Switzerland, this dish is served, as an example, with a Bernese platter. In Heilbronn, Franconia, a casserole is ready for the dish alternately with coarse liver pudding and mashed potatoes in a baking dish so well baked within the oven until the highest layer of mashed potatoes turn slightly brown. To do this, bread and/or Schupfnudeln are enough. Lastly, Klunz may be a Central German variation with lard.

27. ZIGEUNERSCHNITZEL AKA (POLITICALLY INCORRECT) – "GYPSY SCHNITZEL"

Now here is a delicious addition, as well as a poignant 'win' for the 'PC Era' (politically correct era) of our modern times. This delight is a briefly cooked Wiener schnitzel with the historical incorrectness in the name 'Zigeunerschnitzel' is standard in German and Austrian culinary arts. It is sometimes served with a sauce flavored with paprika, tomatoes, mushrooms and alternative ingredients if necessary. Of course, the most effective and often used side dish for this is 'pommes frites' - French fries!

Breaded pork Wiener schnitzel with 'Zigeunersauce' (gypsy sauce) are usually offered as 'Zigeunerschnitzel'. Historically, it is additionally offered with a white sauce. Within the abundant and simplified version of the preparation that remains glorious in the modern world nowadays, pork Wiener schnitzel is sometimes floured or breaded, then cooked. During this variant, the sauce forever includes finely shredded sweet peppers that may be enriched with mushrooms and onions. This is often followed by fixings or ketchup, red wine, broth, and 'Ajvar'. Zigeunerschnitzel features a permanent place on the menus of Central Europe takeaways, as is mostly the case in restaurants and institutions with fast food.

The term "gypsy" (Zigeuner) is more and more rejected in Germany. As an alternate term for the dish, the terms 'paprika schnitzel', that within the cooks' nomenclature already describes another basic formula - 'Balkan schnitzel'.

After a Sinti and Roma forum in Hanover asked the makers of 'gypsy sauces' to rename them as a result of the term being deemed discriminatory, correctly so, in the late summer of 2013, the town of Hanover set to now not supply the dish in its urban canteens under the name of 'gypsy' Wiener schnitzel, but instead as "Schnitzel Balkan-style" or "Schnitzel Budapest-style". The 'PC Era' wins the day!

28. EIERSALAT (EGG SALAD)

I can only assume that there must be so many variations of this dish to name, so let's keep it simple, and let's keep it German.

Egg dishes may be considered more than a breakfast dish. This one consists of hard-boiled, crushed eggs, that are mixed with alternative ingredients in an exceeding mayonnaise or yummy food sauce. Typical spices are common salt, pepper, cayenne pepper, juice, and mustard.

29. HORSE-MEAT SALAMI

This is a seriously delicate addition to the many regional Christmas markets (Weihnachtsmarkt) in Germany during the holidays. I have never personally tried this myself because of my own personal inhibitions when it comes to eating the flesh of a horse. The horse, and the consuming of its flesh, comes with a taboo to some, or maybe even for many. Horse meat was historically employed in the Rhenish dish. Since the meat of recent horses was robust, it had to be softened by the stain. However, since the provision and consumption of horse meat have thankfully declined sharply in recent decades, it's currently principally made up of beef. The sauce is ready regionally otherwise with or without raisins, a part of the marinade and sweeteners to grant it the specified sweet and bitter style. Historically sweeteners are sugar beet sweetening, apple cabbage, Aachener Printen or cake. The pastries additionally serve to bind the sauce rather than or along with flour or starch.

Classic facet dishes to the Rhenish dish are potato dumplings and apple sauce, usually served with poached potatoes or food and red cabbage, additionally seldom made with baked fruit. The 'Pepse', not to be confused with the beverage, and also 'Rheinische Pepse', can be a pork dish within the Rhenish means. During this preparation, one ideally uses a chunk of the pork leg or shoulder.

The Baden dish primarily differs from the Rheinischer dish within the virtually exclusive use of beef and therefore the lack of sweeteners like sugar beet sweetening. Also, no raisins are added to the Badischer dish, which supplies the dish an additional acidic character than the Rheinischer dish. A part of the stain is employed for the sauce, which is sometimes thickened with flour, cake or a gently cooked mixture.

The meat marinates for a minimum of every week within the stain, during which numerous spices like garlic, cloves, mustard seeds, laurel, onions and coriander seeds [6] or cake are used as a spice substitute. the employment of garlic and cake spice differentiates the Baden dish from several alternative regional variants. typically the vinegar for the stain is replaced by dry wine or mixed with it. The stain is so stronger in style and color. Spätzle and red cabbage ar historically served with the Baden dish. alternative cabbage vegetables or differing kinds of dumplings additionally function a dish.

30. ZWIEBELKUCHEN (ONIONCAKE)

The onion cake is popular within the south and east of Germany, where it is commonly enjoyed with a glass of Federweißer and is incredibly simple to bake yourself. It's very healthy, and many of my fellow African friends and colleagues seem to gravitate to this originally African idea.

In Germany, it is sometimes a square or spherical sheet cake made up of yeast dough or a cake supported shortcrust pastry that's equivalent to 'quiche Lorraine'. Speaking of the onions, which are added with soured cream or sweet cream, eggs and bacon cubes are usually used for the topping.

In distinction to the tarte flambée, the onions are sometimes not prepared raw, however, one can take tiny onions and steam them in butter or in the grease from the bacon used for the topping before its' being applied to the dough. Then they are mixed with the remaining ingredients and the mass is finally seasoned with salt and caraway seeds. The caraway ought to contribute to the higher edibleness of the onion cake. Onions are given a personality of sorts with this dish, so what would these onions prefer?

Especially in the geographic region of Anhalt and Saxony, neither onions nor bacon ar cooked beforehand, however, if one were to place it directly onto the dough so poured on with a mass of egg and soured cream, then if left free once baking, the raw onions prefer an extended baking time, and then the topping is usually thicker than style in southern Germany.

Onion cakes are offered particularly in the time of year at the urban center onion market and wine festivals in German wine-growing regions - as an example in Baden, on the Rhine, Mosel, Saar (there as Zwiwwelkuche or Quiche) and Nahe, within the Pfalz, in the winter or Franconia. This onion-cake likes to be eaten warm; when cooling, it may be referred to a temperature within the microwave, added in parts. New wine, sometimes Federweißer, might be an ancient companion. Wine, as an example, a dry Riesling, or numerous forms of this brewage are very appropriate as an associate attendant drink.

31. EISBEIN (KNUCKLE)

Eisbein (Pork knuckle) in lager sauce is a conventional formula from Bavarian cooking. It is very popular during Oktoberfest. I have experienced this dish at least twice, and the second turn was more memorable perhaps because I added a huge glass of Pils beer to it, so maybe that makes a difference. Oktoberfest is considered a good time to drink a beer. Some would argue that "anytime" is "Miller time". Be that as it may, Eisbein is likewise a happy dinner treat during Advent. Zesty bread dumplings and some red cabbage go flawlessly with it.

Eisbein (actually: "ice leg") is made of salted ham sell, typically relieved and marginally bubbled. The word originates from the bone which was once utilized for sharp edges of ice skates. In the Southern regions of Germany, regular readiness is known as Schweinshaxe, and it is normally simmered. Eisbein is normally sold previously relieved and at times smoked, and afterward utilized in straightforward generous dishes. Various local varieties exist, for instance in Berlin it is presented with pease pudding.

In Franconia, Eisbein is usually presented with pureed potatoes or sauerkraut, in Austria with horseradish and mustard.

32. BIENENSTICH (BEESTING)

Regardless of the name of this delectable baked good and where it originates from, we know one thing most importantly, in particular, that it is extremely scrumptious and goes so well with a crisply blended mug of espresso-Americano. Customarily, the "honeybee sting" comprises of yeast mixture with a covering of a fat-sugar-almond mass that caramelizes when heated. All things considered, if that doesn't seem like a tasty quick snack!

Ingredients for 1 serving:
For the ground:
500 g   Flour
250 ml milk
1 cube yeast
75 g Butter, soft
75 g sugar
1 pinch (s) salt

For covering:

150 g   butter
100 g   sugar
2 tbsp   honey
4 tbsp   cream
250 g   Flaked almonds
For the cream:
1 pack   Custard powder
2 tbsp   sugar
500 ml milk
250 g   Butter, soft

For the mixture, crumble the yeast into 3D shapes and break down them in tepid milk with a whisk. Presently put the yeast milk in a bowl and use flour, sugar, margarine and a spot of salt to cause a smooth batter with a blender first and afterward to ply into a ball with your hands. The batter ball must go secured at room temperature for 30 minutes.

Ply the mixture again on a floured work surface and afterward turn it out on a lubed preparing sheet. Prick with a fork and leave secured again for 30 minutes. Meanwhile, the almond garnish can be readied. To do this, bring the spread, sugar, cream, and nectar to a bubble in a pan and mix in the almond leaves. After the mass has cooled somewhat, it very well may be spread over the yeast mixture. This must be prepared in the preheated broiler at 200° C/392° F top/base warmth for around 20 minutes and afterward cool on a wire rack.

Meanwhile, the pudding cream can be readied. To do this, set up the custard as indicated by the bundle guidelines and let it cool. It is ideal to cover it with a stick film so no skin can shape. At that point mix the delicate spread with the blender until it is smooth white and mix in the pudding, which has cooled to room temperature, in tablespoons.

Quarter the completely cooled cake and cut each quarter equally. Spread the margarine cream on the lower parts and smooth out. Spot various pieces of the prepared great on top and press down tenderly.

Note: It is perfect to put the pieces in the fridge for 30 minutes with the objective that the spread cream sets and the 'honeybee sting' can be cut easily.

33. BIENENSTICH (BEESTING)

Regardless of the name of this delectable baked good and where it originates from, we know one thing most importantly, in particular, that it is extremely scrumptious and goes so well with a crisply blended mug of espresso-Americano. Customarily, the "honey bee sting" comprises of yeast mixture with a covering of a fat-sugar-almond mass that caramelizes when heated. All things considered, if that doesn't seem like a tasty quick snack!

Ingredients for 1 serving:
For the ground:
500 g   Flour
250 ml milk
1 cube yeast
75 g Butter, soft
75 g sugar
1 pinch (s) salt

For covering:

150 g   butter
100 g   sugar
2 tbsp   honey
4 tbsp   cream
250 g   Flaked almonds
For the cream:
1 pack   Custard powder
2 tbsp   sugar
500 ml milk
250 g   Butter, soft

For the mixture, crumble the yeast into 3D shapes and break down them in tepid milk with a whisk. Presently put the yeast milk in a bowl and use flour, sugar, margarine and a spot of salt to cause a smooth batter with a blender first and afterward to ply into a ball with your hands. The batter ball must go secured at room temperature for 30 minutes.

Ply the mixture again on a floured work surface and afterward turn it out on a lubed preparing sheet. Prick with a fork and leave secured again for 30 minutes. Meanwhile, the almond garnish can be readied. To do this, bring the spread, sugar, cream, and nectar to a bubble in a pan and mix in the almond leaves. After the mass has cooled somewhat, it very well may be spread over the yeast mixture. This must be prepared in the preheated broiler at 200° C/392° F top/base warmth for around 20 minutes and afterward cool on a wire rack.

Meanwhile, the pudding cream can be readied. To do this, set up the custard as indicated by the bundle guidelines and let it cool. It is ideal to cover it with a stick film so no skin can shape. At that point mix the delicate spread with the blender until it is smooth white and mix in the pudding, which has cooled to room temperature, in tablespoons.

Quarter the completely cooled cake and cut each quarter equally. Spread the margarine cream on the lower parts and smooth out. Spot various pieces of the prepared great on top and press down tenderly.

Note: It is perfect to put the pieces in the fridge for 30 minutes with the objective that the spread cream sets and the 'honeybee sting' can be cut easily.

34. HERINGSSALAT (HERRING SALAD)

This is for the port-city Captain in us all...the sea-faring voyager who delights in a delicacy of the far north after a midsummer's cruise through the seas and their many beautiful ocean-side towns complete with their very own special lighthouse to guide the ships.

This fishy dish is not solely eaten within the northern regions of Europe and Germany. Whether or not with beetroot, there are various variants for the preparation of this German delicacy. Classic Scandinavian and customary Dutch variations are made with dehydrated herring, poached potatoes, celery, preserved cucumbers, and apples, diced with a thick marinade made up of herring milk, grated onions, vinegar, and oil. For the Dutch herring, the regionally typical 'matjes' is employed as fish. Within the Swedish means, salt-cured herrings, poached beef, beetroot, and apples are mixed with a vinegar and oil marinade, also as shredded anchovies, preserved gherkins, capers, and mustard.

Herring salad in the Northern-German vogue circles of society consists of salt-cured herring, medium meat, beetroot, preserved cucumber, and mayonnaise and features a corresponding red color. In several areas, it's a standard dish on a Christian holy day. Several restaurants supply a lavish fish buffet as a herring feast on such holidays and festivities.

35. JÄGERSCHNITZEL (HUNTER'S SCHNITZEL)

Until the day that I decided to cut pork products from my diet was the day that I replaced my usual Jägerschnitzel cooked with ham and I have vied for the one with turkey or veal instead, though very rarely. This used to be my favorite food, right up there with the common ones like chicken, pizza, or popcorn for some. This one almost became addictively good to me, but I have since recovered. I am Mikael Arcangeli, and I was a 'Jägerschnitzelaholic'. I confess it is seriously that good.

Jägerschnitzel is an exemplary food dish produced using seared veal or pork schnitzel with a mushroom-tomato or mushroom-cream sauce. Provincially, a schnitzel produced using breaded, seared hotdog with tomato sauce and pasta is otherwise called a hunter's schnitzel.

For the 'exemplary planning', veal escalopes are seared without breading. For the sauce, shallots are sweat soaked, deglazed with white wine, overflowed with force and, as indicated by certain plans, added with tomato sauce and completed with steamed mushrooms, chanterelles, and morels. In a variation, quickly singed pork cutlets are braised in sharp cream with broiled onions, chanterelles, and peppers. Great side dishes are French fries, fried potatoes, pasta or rice.

36. KARTOFFELSUPPE (POTATO SOUP)

Potato soup warms and fills the body particularly in the winter months. Each leisure activity and gourmet specialist cook most likely has his or her

formula. There are various plans and the arrangement
is different territorially. The potatoes, perhaps
together with different vegetables, for example,
carrots, celery, and onions are cooked in saltwater or
juices.

The regularly accessible vegetables are for the
most part well utilized. After the cooking procedure,
the potatoes are squashed or pounded with a potato
masher. Contingent upon the recipe, the soup
accompanies singed bacon shapes or seared onions
and crisp parsley. Different herbs and peppers are
utilized as flavors.

Bockwurst, Wieners, meatballs, Leberwurst,
Blutwurst, Jagdwurst or different kinds of meat or
meat arrangements are regularly served with the
potato soup. A cut of bread or rolls is frequently
filled in as a side dish, some of which are soared into
the soup. In northern Germany, potato soup in
marginally unique territorial varieties is a piece of the
standard collection of home cooking. Known among
others are the Mecklenburg strong Tüffel un Plum
(Low German: "potatoes and plums"), likewise
Tüften un Plum or Mecklenburg potato soup, which is
set up from potatoes, vegetables and diced Kassler

neck or bacon and with prunes. This is regularly a unique preference for Mecklenburg and Schleswig-Holstein food, and here is the connection of an exceptionally salted thus zesty potato and meat stew dish with a sweet supplement.

In Baden cooking, particularly in southern Baden and on the focal Upper Rhine - increasingly more popular in the Karlsruhe region, potato soup is a territorial strength as a potato soup with plum cake. In the Pfalz and the Saarland, as well, cranberry soup is generally eaten with crush cake or potato soup with steamed noodles. In parts of Swabia, a crusty fruit-filled treat is eaten with the potato soup.

In certain districts of the Vorderpfalz and Rheinhessen, a variation of the potato soup is additionally called "Saurie Brieh" (harsh stock). The potatoes quickly simmered with onions and garlic are cooked on a low fire in clear pork juices until they have disintegrated. This sort of cooking compares to the Portuguese "caldo verde". This smooth soup is prepared with vinegar and presented with a spoon of boiled blood and liver hotdog (Blut-und Leberwurst).

37. JAGDWURST

Jagdwurst is my favorite variation of the hunter's schnitzel that started in the German Democratic Republic depends on inventiveness because of an absence of fixings. I personally experienced eating this dish by accident in an old-timey German hotel that was complete with a narrow set of stairs (it was actually more like a ladder) leading to my room which was located in an attic. This kind of "coziness" had me spending a majority of my time in the hotel restaurant, which was surprisingly exquisite, and that was how I met "Herr Jagdwurst". In times when cultivated meat was a rare thing, it was simpler to get singed hotdogs, for example, brew ham from the remaining parts of destroyed meat or pork stomach. For readiness, the wiener is cut into finger-thick cuts, breaded and singed until firm in cooking oil or explained margarine. For the sauce, tomatoes or tomato paste with onions and conceivably bacon skin is steamed, add roux and water and cook everything to a rich sauce. The bacon skin is added before serving. The typical side dishes are pasta, potatoes, pureed potatoes, French fries or a serving of mixed greens. It's the kind of food that one might expect to eat at a sporting event.

38. HIMMEL UND ERDE (HEAVEN AND EARTH)

Himmel und Erde is a conventional German dish produced using pureed potatoes and fruit purée, which is frequently presented with singed Blutwurst (blood frankfurter), bacon or seared Leberwurst (liver hotdog) and generally famous in the locales of the Rhineland, Westphalia and Lower Saxony. It was additionally well known in the past in Silesia. The dish comprises of dark pudding, singed onions, and squashed potato with fruit purée. It has been around since the 18th century.

The name of the dish begins from the name of two of the primary fixings: the apples originating from the trees, for example from up in the sky, and the potatoes originating starting from the earliest stage. (A tongue word in German for potato is Erdapfel (English: earth apple), or Äädappel in the Rhineland, so there are two sorts of "apples" in the dish).

In certain districts of the Vorderpfalz and Rheinhessen, a variation of the potato soup is additionally called "Saurie Brieh" (sharp stock). The potatoes quickly broiled with onions and garlic are cooked on a low fire in clear pork juices until they have broken down. This kind of cooking compares to the Portuguese caldo verde. This smooth soup is prepared with vinegar and presented with a spoon of cooked blood and liver wiener. (Blut-und Leberwurst).

39. KOHLRABI

Kohlrabi impresses with its particularly delicate taste. In combination with spicy minced meat, a great classical composition of delight is created that tastes truly gourmet! So, pull out your work mittens and elbow grease, because you're going to build up a serious appetite during the preparation of this popular and healthy German delight.

Peel kohlrabi and cook in boiling salted water for about 25 minutes.

Cut the onions into small cubes and knead with minced meat, egg, breadcrumbs, salt & pepper. Scare off the kohlrabi and hollow it out with a teaspoon.

Pat dry well inside with salt and pepper.

Fill minced meat.

Sprinkle with Parmesan, put in a mold, white wine & broth.

Cook in a preheated oven at 180°C/ 356° F (fan oven) for about 30-40 minutes.

Remove kohlrabi from the brew.

Brew through a sieve in a saucepan, bring to the boil, thicken with sauce binders & season with salt, pepper & nutmeg.

40. ROTE GRÜTZE (RED FRUIT JELLY)

One of the most delicious German desserts is red fruit jelly with vanilla sauce. The mixed berry composite also tastes great with vanilla ice cream or on a warm portion of rice pudding.

To create this delight, it's extremely easy and time savory. You'll need:

1 glass of morello cherries

1 small glass of cranberries

1 pack of frozen berry mix

1 packet of vanilla sugar

Your own amount of cornstarch

Mix the vanilla sugar and the cornstarch with the juice of the cherries.

Put everything in a saucepan, bring to the boil for a moment, and that's it!

41. SCHUPFNUDELN (POTATO NOODLES)

Schupfnudeln is super easy to make yourself and it tastes particularly good with sauerkraut and bacon. It's very popular in Germany. I've seen it added as a side dish to the main course of many lunches and dinners in Germany as almost equally that I've witnessed hamburgers on plates with a side of fries.

Wash the potatoes and cook in simmering water until they are soft. Peel them while they're still warm and press through a potato ricer. Spread onto a baking sheet and set aside to allow the water to evaporate. Once cooled, knead the egg and flour into

the potatoes. Season with salt and nutmeg, and form
into a long, thin roll. Cut into one-inch pieces and
use your hands to form bite-sized, finger-shaped
dumplings by rolling them with your palms.

Cook them in lightly boiling salted water until they
come to the top. Take out with a skimmer and leave
to cool a bit. Melt the butter in a pan. Add some sage
leaves and wait for them to become crispy. Add the
dumplings and sauté for 5-10 minutes until golden
brown. 'Easy peasy'…

42. KARTOFFELBREI (MASHED POTATOES)

One of the most popular German side dishes is
Kartoffelbrei. I think that it tastes the best
homemade.

We love to make these creamy mashed potatoes at
home pretty often. In this method of preparation, we
started with a classic potato porridge recipe and
refined it with some mustard, which seriously adds a
refreshing note. I'd go as far as to say that I've
become so accustomed to this little addition to the

mashed potatoes that I still, to this writing, ask for mustard at restaurants to serve with my potatoes. They go together like peas and carrots. To feed a family of four, as an example, you will need:

750 g of floury potatoes
25 g butter
80 ml milk
Coarse salt for the cooking process
nutmeg
Sea salt and pepper from the mill
Mustard (as desired)

43. GERMAN CHEESECAKE

There is a big difference between the highly sweet and addicting cheesecake styles of New York, Boston, or the extremely sweet Key West variety, and German cheesecake. Your kids won't annoy you to death due to being so hyperactive from this particular cheesecake variety. This is a wonderful, a bit juicy, and much milder cheesecake that once you can allow yourself to become accustomed to, you can never get enough of this homemade cheesecake. Unlike its

American cousin, this variety of cheesecake doesn't taste too sweet and has a wonderfully light consistency. It's really good with a nice espresso, or even a glass of mid-range red wine. This dish I would not recommend trying to whip up yourself. The best experience, if one can get as far as Germany or Austria, Switzerland or Italy, would be to request this dessert in a nice café or restaurant, or the experience of enjoying this treat might well become null and void. To make some comical sense of this observation, imagine going trick-or-treating… in your own home?

44. FRANKFURT GREEN SAUCE

Yummy, healthy and fresh - that's the Frankfurt Green Sauce. Seven herbs, a lucky number, are used for this preparation. It is usually eaten with boiled potatoes and hard-boiled eggs or with schnitzel. You will need:

200 g herbs
mixed for Frankfurt Green Sauce
fresh
200 g sour cream

(sour cream) 10% fat
1 kg of natural yogurt
2.8% fat
1 tsp sugar
1 tsp heaped mustard
1 tsp heaped salt
6 pieces of egg (s)
cooked hard

45. GERMKNÖDEL

Germ dumplings (also called yeast dumplings)
with a sweet filling are a specialty in southern
Germany and Austria. This recipe is traditionally
filled with plums and sprinkled with poppy seeds.
You'll need:

200 ml milk
20 g yeast (cubes)
500g flour
5 tablespoons of sugar
150 g butter
1 egg
1 pinch of salt

grated zest of 1 lemon

8 tsp of plum jam

150 ml water

50 g poppy seeds

Warm-up half of the milk until it is lukewarm. Add yeast and dissolve. Put flour in a separate bowl and form a hollow in the middle. Add the yeast and milk, add 1 tablespoon of sugar and stir well. Leave covered for 15 minutes. Melt 50 g of the butter and mix with the remaining 100 ml of milk.

Add this mixture with egg, salt, 1 tablespoon of sugar and lemon zest to the previous dough from step 2 and stir well. Cover again and let go for 30 minutes. Knead well and divide into 8 balls, press flat. Put a teaspoon of plum jam on each flatbread and shape it into dumplings. Sprinkle flour on a baking sheet, place the dumplings on top and leave covered at 50 ° C for 20 minutes.

Boil 150 ml of water and place three dumplings next to each other in a steam insert. Steam over low heat for up to 25 minutes.

Take out the dumplings, insert them and keep them warm on a greased tray. Prepare the remaining dumplings in the same way.

Melt 100 g butter and mix with the poppy seeds and the remaining 3 tablespoons of sugar, pour over the finished dumplings.

46. MÖHRENEINTOPF

A great winter dish is carrot stew, which is easy to prepare and quick to cook.

You need:

2 kg of carrots
12 medium-sized potatoes
2 onions
1 apple
500 ml vegetable broth
salt and pepper
maybe some butter
Peel the vegetables and apple and cook in the vegetable stock. Then stomp with a pounder, if

necessary, pour some of the excess water beforehand so that the stew does not become too liquid.

Salt, pepper and add a little butter if necessary. This goes great with cabbage sausage.

47. DRESDNER EIERSCHECKE

The name Dresdner Eierschecke (literally "Dresden egg pinto") hides a delicious cake with curd cheese and custard. It is super quick and easy to bake. You will need:

700g curd cheese
2 eggs
1 pack of custard
200g sugar
For the second mass:
375ml milk
100g sugar
1 pack of custard
100g butter
5 eggs

Mix the ingredients for the first mass and pour it into a greased springform pan. Warning: Do not cook the custard, just add the powder. Cook a pudding from milk, sugar, and custard and let it cool. Mix the butter and 5 egg yolks until frothy and mix into the pudding. Finally beat the egg whites until stiff, fold into the second mixture and fill in the springform pan. Bake everything at about 175° C/ 347° F for about one hour.

48. DONAUWELLE

This dessert is a biscuit base with yummy sour cherries, creamy filling, and delicious chocolate glaze. The Germans, from my experience and perspective, normally get pretty excited about Donauwelle. I also like it myself. You'll need:

Batter
2 eq. Sour cherries (drained weight 350 g each)
250 g soft margarine or butter
200 g of sugar
1 pack of vanillin sugar
1 pr. Salt

5 eggs (size M)

375 g of wheat flour

3 tsp baking soda

20 g cocoa

1 tablespoon milk

Buttercream:

1 pack of pudding powder vanilla flavor

100 g of sugar

500 ml of milk

250 g soft butter

Molding:

200 g dark chocolate

2 tablespoons of cooking oil

e.g. B. sunflower oil

49. SEMMELKNÖDEL

Unlike the potato dumplings already mentioned, bread dumplings are made from stale bread. A great accompaniment to all kinds of dishes, not just roast goose, this dish is very common in the south of Germany. I have lived and worked primarily in the south-western area of Germany.

Peel the onion and chop it finely. Then chop the fresh parsley very evenly and fine. Crumble the bread and add the eggs to the bread, onions, and parsley. Add the vegetable broth. Mix all ingredients well. It's best to use your hands for this, it's also more fun;)

Then season the dumpling dough with a little salt and pepper. Let it sit in a bowl covered with a kitchen towel, handrag, or thick paper towel for about an hour.

50. METTIGEL

Last, and certainly not least, I am adding one of the most curious dishes of this entire book - the Mettigel. I can assure the fantasy and adventure fans that "Mettigel" is not a nickname that stands for a guard-post of Orks and goblins to go forth with your team of elves and dwarfs to go and "beef" with. Speaking of beef, the raw meat is mixed with chopped onions and parsley, formed into a hedgehog and spiked with onion strips as spikes. The strange party snack is very healthy when high-quality and farm-fresh meat is used. It is an acquired taste, like any good ethnic delicacy, so now we are getting deep into some serious and popular Central European 'delicatessen'.

For the conventional preparations, a huge bit of molded is molded into the shape of a hedgehog and adorned with pretzel sticks or crude quartered onion rings as "spikes" and olives or the like as "eyes" and "nose". It is regularly served on a bed of lettuce leaves, crude cleaved onions or onion rings. These are bread, buns or pretzels and spread with pepper and salt enough for any flavoring to one's taste. Because of the perishability of minced meat, the Mettigel ought to be eaten upon the arrival of assembling, so don't let this one just sits there out in the open for a while. A tantamount dish is cheddar hedgehogs.

Serving cold plates with Mettigel became stylish during the 1950s. Like toadstool eggs and tomatoes, cheddar sticks with grapes, cheddar hedgehogs or ham rolls and packs, it was a piece of the standard collection of cold smorgasbords, particularly in private parties, until the 1970s. It was frequently served with locally brewed beer, bread, and butter.

This is the only addition to this book that I have actually not tried myself, so I cannot accuse this dish, nor can I confirm nor deny, of its tastiness or ghastliness. I have seen this delicacy on the tables of many artists' buffets backstage and/or in the salons of the Baroque style castles and chateaus. I always felt particularly rude whenever I would gesture to politely decline the Mettigel, but I just couldn't get over the idea of eating raw meat for reasons that I cannot explain to this writing. I'll end these festivities with that thought in your mind; and maybe, just maybe, you, the reader could enlighten me someday as to if I'm rude, or just being too honest...

READ OTHER BOOKS BY CZYK PUBLISHING

Greater Than a Tourist- St. Croix US Birgin Islands USA: 50 Travel Tips from a Local by Tracy Birdsall

Greater Than a Tourist- Toulouse France: 50 Travel Tips from a Local by Alix Barnaud

Children's Book: *Charlie the Cavalier Travels the World* by Lisa Rusczyk

Eat Like a Local

Follow *Eat Like a Local on* Amazon.
Join our mailing list for new books
http://bit.ly/EatLikeaLocalbooks

Printed in Great Britain
by Amazon

23219026R00067